Agricultural Journalism

NIPA® GENX ELECTRONIC RESOURCES & SOLUTIONS P. LTD.
New Delhi-110 034

About the Authors

Dr. Debasmita Nayak graduated from Odisha University of Agriculture and Technology, Bhubaneswar. She has obtained her master's and Ph.D degree in Extension Education from College of Agriculture, OUAT, Bhubaneswar. She has extensive experience working as an assistant professor and instructing undergraduate students. She is currently working as an Assistant Professor in Sri Sri University, Cuttack, Odisha. She has been awarded by different professional societies including young Research fellow award- 2020, Young Scientist Award-2023. She has published many research papers, book chapters and popular articles in various reputed national and international journals.

Mrs. Mita Meher graduated from Odisha University of Agriculture and Technology, Bhubaneswar. She earned her master's degree in Extension Education with distinction standing first in order of merit from College of Agriculture, OUAT, Bhubaneswar and currently pursuing Ph.D. from Indira Gandhi Krishi Viswavidyalaya, Raipur. She has a vast experience of teaching to Undergraduate students as an Assistant Professor. She has been conferred with several awards by different professional societies including PG Research Award- 2020, Young Scientist Award in Agricultural Extension-2022, Young Scientist Award-2023. She has published many research papers, book chapters and popular articles in various reputed national and international journals.

Agricultural Journalism

Debasmita Nayak
Mita Meher

NIPA® GENX ELECTRONIC RESOURCES & SOLUTIONS P. LTD.
New Delhi-110 034

NIPA® GENX ELECTRONIC
RESOURCES & SOLUTIONS P. LTD.

101,103, Vikas Surya Plaza, CU Block
L.S.C.Market, Pitam Pura, New Delhi-110 034
Ph : +91 11 27341616, 27341717, 27341718
E-mail: newindiapublishingagency@gmail.com
www: www.nipabooks.com

For customer assistance, please contact
Phone: + 91-11-27 34 17 17
Fax: + 91-11-27 34 16 16
E-Mail: feedbacks@nipabooks.com

ISBN: 978-93-58872-92-7

Composed and Designed by NIPA.

Preface

Modern society depends on journalism and communications because they inform and educate the public about a wide range of subjects and events. It is essential for influencing public opinion and building a progressive, educated society.

Agricultural journalism is an important tool for communicating with farmers, homemakers, and others. Newspaper stories, magazine articles, leaflets, pamphlets, bulletins, circular letters, wall newspapers and radio scripts are increasingly being written and read or listened to by extension staff. The book contains the procedure of agricultural story writing, Headline writing, Lay-outing, Caption writing, Gathering information etc.

The authors of this book would like to express their gratitude to their family, teachers and friends.

The authors of this book would also like to thanks the NIPA publication for the support.

Authors

Contents

1

Journalism

The word journalism is derived from the word "Journal" which means a daily register or a diary.

- Journalism is the written, spoken, or visual dissemination of information about a day's events.
- A journalist is someone who works as a writer or editor for a newspaper or magazine.
- Father of journalism: **Joseph Pulitzer**
- Father of journalism in India: **James Augustus Hicky**

(Joseph Pulitzer) Source: Internet

(James Augustus Hicky) Source:Internet

Meaning

- The process of acquiring, analysing, producing, and presenting news and information is known as journalism.
- Journalism is that area of social interaction that is concerned with the communication of information and opinions about society. Five departments of mass communication are the part of contemporary journalism. (1) Print media, (2) Radio, (3) Television, (4) Motion pictures, and (5) Advertising.

Definition

- Welsley (1969) defined journalism as the systematic and reliable gathering, writing, interpreting, processing and disseminating of public opinion, public information and public entertainment for publication in news papers, magazines and telecast.
- According to Bond F. Fraser "The term journalism embraces all the forms in which and through which the news and the comments on the news reach the public. All that happens in the world, if such happenings hold interest for the public and all the thought, action and ideas which these happenings stimulate become the basic material for the journalist."
- According to Leslie Stephens, "Journalism consists of writing for pay on matters of which you are ignorant."

Importance of Journalism

- It informs and disseminates information: It is essentially information communication. The daily events are disseminated through a few words, sounds, pictures, and so on to satisfy people's curiosity about the environment and the world. People become more aware of various fields such as politics, history, laws, science, geography, socioeconomic aspects, sex, crime, violence, racial conflict, and so on as a result of the news.
- It educates the people: The various media of journalism play an important role in providing a wide range of information on topics such as health and sanitation, laws, cultural aspects such as customs, traditions, norms, and so on, and other human activities. In a developing country like India, where 35% of the population is illiterate, journalism plays an important role in educating them through the use of audio-visual aids. These media aid in changing people's knowledge, skills, attitudes, values, norms, understandings, and beliefs in the desired direction.
- It provides entertainment opportunities: People are entertained by the various media of journalism through various programs such as publishing feature, humour, comics, fictions, and broadcasting / telecasting music, songs, dances, and so on.
- It shapes public opinion and thinking by delivering social or commercial messages: It provides information on events by presenting various facts about the past, present, and future. It directs people's thoughts by discussing the truth, problems, potential solutions, and potential consequences of a specific event or thing. It serves as a watchdog over people's thoughts and expression, allowing them to express themselves freely through journalism.
- It contributes to the preservation of democracy: The news and related information of parliament and legislature are disseminated throughout the country via the media of journalism. People can reach out to the government through various media outlets when it comes to elections and other related issues. It also aids in the fight against injustice to a specific group, community, or strain. It also aids in voting and other decision-making processes.
- It aids in the development of national identity: These media outlets disseminate news and non-news about national and international issues throughout the country. The exchange of ideas, facts, and scientific information in various fields aids in the development of national identity. It also contributes to national unity and integrity by disseminating facts throughout the community and country.

- It serves as an agent in the collection, preservation, and presentation of news and reading matters to various journalistic media: The stock exchange news is now available on computer from a data bank. The electronic or word processing typewriter eliminates the need for retyping drafts and letters. The advancement of electronic and computer technologies has aided in the dissemination and use of information. It aids in the dissemination of information on all underground news as well as current events.

Principles of Journalism

1. Responsibility: A journalist's right is to write and draw readers' attention to issues of public welfare.
2. Sincerity, truthfulness, and accuracy: Readers' trust can be gained through sincerity, truthfulness, and accuracy, which is the foundation of journalism.
3. Objectivity / impartiality: A journalist's basic lesson is to maintain impartiality in reporting; otherwise, readers' reactions to the report will be lopsided.
4. Justice: The proper practice of journalism is to treat the public fairly.
5. Independence: Except for matters of public interest, journalism is free of all obligations.
6. Press freedom: The primary responsibility of journalism is to protect its freedom.
7. Integrity: Journalism attempts to shape public behavior in a given situation.

Basic function of Journalism

1. The information function

The primary purpose of the press is to inform. Newspapermen must assess which public events, ideas, and situations will pique the public's interest. Aside from the factual presentation of news, the complex situation necessitates interpretation and explanation.

2. The opinion function

Modern man frequently finds himself perplexed about which product to buy. What should you do? Who should I vote for? He requires a means of communication that will help him understand the positive and negative aspects of situations through logical arguments. As a result, the modern press must serve as both a daily teacher and a daily tribute. As a result, the editorial is the only way to influence public opinion.

3. The entertainment function

Entertaining the public is the function and a business too. Since it is too big a job for the local staff, newspaper relies upon syndicated materials. Entertainment is where you find it. It pops up in human-interest stories and news features. Public interest in various features, comics in particular sometimes determine the choice of a newspaper.

Types of Journalism

1. Advocacy journalism
2. Interpretative journalism
3. Development journalism in agriculture
4. Convergence journalism
5. Ambush journalism

Advocacy journalism

- Started in USA in early 19th century
- Journalism that adopts a non-objective stance, typically for a social or political objective, is known as advocacy journalism.
- Because of the perceived influence of corporate sponsors in advertising, some advocacy journalists reject the idea that the traditional ideal of objectivity is possible or practical. Proponents of advocacy journalism believe that a diverse range of media outlets with opposing viewpoints serves the public interest better, or that advocacy journalism serves a similar function to muckraking.

Interpretative journalism

- A journalist must go beyond simply reporting the essential details of an event in order to engage in interpretive journalism or interpretive reporting. The practise of interpretative journalism overlaps with a number of other journalism genres as a result of the lack of clear boundaries and the diversity of theoretical approaches related to what interpretative journalism is in the modern world.

Development journalism in agriculture

- According to the definition of development journalism, it is "a style of reporting and writing on subjects relevant to the process of economic development."
- It emphasises the development and protection of the rural community.

- The approaches range from development journalists acting as willing partners of the government (statist) to watchdogs (investigative) and interventionist (participatory or emancipatory) to transparency guardians. There are more variants or combinations within the range. On the plus side, there is agreement on some essentials for development journalism, such as the emphasis on the process of development to bring about social change (communitarian).

Convergence journalism

- Convergence journalism is a subset of journalism that combines different media types (such as writing, video, photographs, and more) to produce a bigger editorial endeavour.
- Media convergence and the digital devices that enable it are typically classified into several types in order to describe the various phenomena observed as part of the media convergence process. Technological convergence, economic convergence, and cultural convergence are three important aspects of media convergence.

Ambush journalism

- Ambush journalism is the method through which a news reporter approaches an unwilling person in an unexpected setting, such as a sidewalk or parking lot, to ask them questions and get spontaneous answers.

Other types

Photo-journalism

In this kind, pictures are utilised to tell stories. Sometimes the pictures tell the story on their own, and other times they are just employed to bolster the written narrative.

Feature journalism

Featured stories are typically the kind that take longer to develop than regular stories. A feature is put together using a great deal more investigation and comprehensive data gathering.

Tabloid journalism

This is sensationalised news; certain aspects of it have been deftly altered. This style of reporting is also referred to as "yellow journalism," and the material it contains is not entirely trustworthy.

Parachute journalism

This approach necessitates travelling to many locations throughout the globe to obtain data. This is a difficult way to gather news in journalism because the journalist may frequently find himself in an alien environment, in a foreign nation, working in difficult conditions, and working under pressure.

Drone journalism

As the name implies, in this style of journalism, news is obtained using a tool called a drone. These drones are used to gather images, videos, and news. A drone is the most effective means to acquire information in the event of conflict, natural disasters, etc.

Gotcha journalism

It's a difficult method of learning the news. It calls for a great deal of subtlety and expert precision. By asking the source in a way that the sensitive questions are addressed on their own, the information is acquired using this technique. This method is employed for conducting interviews about contentious issues.

Participatory journalism

People who use this strategy provide as a forum for discussions and disputes and serve as information sources. It resembles citizen journalism quite a bit.

Collaborative journalism

In this approach, numerous news outlets and independent journalists collaborate to produce a single large piece of news or to share the multiple smaller pieces of the news that they have the legal right to with one another and produce their own unique stories out of it.

Scope

The current public extension system cannot satisfy the farmers' informational needs since they are information-hungry. The ratio of extension agents to farmers is growing. On the other hand, communication tools are rapidly developing. Additionally, private extension is becoming a factor. With media tycoons often launching new channels, journals, and publishing firms, journalism has a lot of potential in India today. Since there is so much competition, every newspaper and channel tries to provide something unique, which has in turn given the viewer a wide range of options.

History of development of print media in India

- 1550: 1st Printing Press in India.
- Only religious texts were initially published in Portuguese, Tamil, and Malayalam.
- In Calcutta, William Bolt made the first effort at newspaper printing. However, **James Augustus** Hicky really founded the first newspaper, the "Bengal Gazette," in Calcutta. The East India Company's servants' private lives are made public in the paper.
- 1784: "Calcutta Gazette" was started.
- 1785: Richard Johnson started the "Madras Courier" from Madras.
- 1789: "Bombay Herald" was started in Bombay. It publishes the personal grievances of the Englishmen against the East India Company.
- 1832: "Bombay Samachar" in Gujrati published from Bombay.
- 1838: "Times of India" in English published from Bombay.
- 1885: 'Pioneer in English" published from Lucknow.
- 1886, "Amrit Bazar Patrika" in English published from Calcutta.

HICKY's
BENGAL GAZETTE;
OR THE ORIGINAL
Calcutta General Advertifer.

(Front page of Hicky's Bengal Gazette, 10 March 1781, from the University of Heidelberg's archive

2

Agricultural Journalism

Definition

Agricultural journalism is a specialized branch of journalism that deals with the techniques of receiving, writing, editing and reporting from information through the media like newspapers, periodicals, radio, TV, advertising etc. and the management processes connected with such production. It is the timely reporting and editing with words and photography of agricultural news and information for newspaper, magazine, radio and television.

It is otherwise known as Farm journalism

Farm journalism is very important for communicating with farm people. More and more of the extension staff's writing is being read or listened to in newspapers, magazines, brochures, pamphlets, bulletins, circular letters, wall newspapers, and radio scripts. The written work makes working as a consultant with farmers more fascinating.

Principles of Farm/Agricultural journalism

1. **Select Facts**

   While selecting facts, the following point are important.

   - Suitable subject matter: Does it satisfy a need? Is this timely? Is it still relevant right now?
   - Readers: Who are the people being targeted? What are their issues, hobbies, and degrees of education? Do they have the right circumstances and the ability to use the information?
   - Purpose of Publication: What do you hope it will accomplish and teach? Do you want to encourage people to watch a show or do you want to persuade them to do an action?

2. **Sift Facts**

   - Sort the important information needed to provide it clearly.
   - Filter out complex ideas

- Instead of a thorough explanation, give the layman an application of the topic.
- Do not document everything.

3. **Sort facts**
   - Put the facts in a logical sequence.
4. **ABC's of Journalism**
   - Accuracy
   - Brevity
   - Clarity
5. **Adopt the following Tips for Readability**
   - Short sentences
   - Simple words
   - Personal or human - interest words.

Role of Agricultural Journalism in Agricultural Development

- Agricultural Journalism raises awareness and combats ignorance by transferring ideas from one person to others.
- It contributes to reducing the knowledge gap that exists between the degree of research findings made available at agricultural research stations and their actual adoption and use by farmers.
- It quickly disseminates the scientific technologies from agricultural research stations to the farming community through a variety of mediums.
- The responsibilities of an agricultural journalist include tasks that help to effectively communicate new agricultural information so that it results in effective application and adoption.
- The main goal of agricultural extension education is to improve the knowledge, skills, attitudes, understanding, activeness, involvement in developmental activities, participation, and psychology of farmers and rural residents; this can only be accomplished through communication. Interaction between the people and the communicator, such as a journalist is communication.

Scope of Agricultural Journalism

- The current public extension system cannot satisfy the farmers' informational needs. The ratio of extension agents to farmers is growing. On the other hand, communication tools are rapidly developing.

- Additionally, private extension is becoming a factor. With media tycoons often launching new channels, journals, and publishing firms, journalism has a lot of potential in India today. Since there is so much rivalry, every newspaper and channel try to develop something unique, which has given the public a tonne of diversity.

Opportunities of Agricultural Journalism

- Creation of new jobs.
- Provide timely information to the community.
- National development.
- Food sufficiency and security.
- Improve the socioeconomic status of the local people.
- Reduce disparities between people.
- Raise the educational level of the society.
- People's empowerment.

Merits of Agricultural Journalism

- Can educate, integrate, and inspire the audience.
- Capable of reaching a large number of people in a short period of time.
- Capable of reaching an audience in difficult-to-reach areas.
- Has the potential to improve public opinion.
- Published print material can be kept for future reference.
- Low cost of mass production (despite a high initial investment)

Prospects in Agricultural Journalism

It gives scientists/extension workers/agriculturalists/farmers more radio and newspaper space to "talk" or "write" directly about their work in order to promote more synergy and collaboration between the two groups.

Be more sensitive to 'gender' in broadcasting and journalism, as rural women are frequently invisible or marginalized in the media despite playing a critical role in rural development.

Establish 'agricultural information centers' at the village level, with the goal of creating platforms where "communities can document their knowledge, listen, and learn together." More efforts should be made to include the media in networks, collaborations, and multistakeholder platforms.

Development organizations should make greater efforts to transport journalists to projects in exchange for increased coverage of agriculture.

To encourage the use of more participatory media, such as participatory radio and video.Use of novel methods for communicating agricultural information. The importance of communitybased FM radio stations and agricultural information centers in providing agricultural information in local languages to rural communities has been repeatedly emphasized, particularly in Africa. Radio is also seen as an important extension tool in the Pacific. However, the following creative examples have also been provided.

Community radio in remote communities is supported by tapes, flyers, and additional information.

The Indian rural press is largely developing, and there is still room for growth.

Literacy in India is increasing on a daily basis.

Journalists' and editors' attitudes toward agricultural messages are also shifting in a positive direction.

The advancement of technology in various media aids in the dissemination of agricultural information to remote areas.

A group of farm journalists is forming.

Problems of Agricultural Journalism

- Low literacy rate
- Less farm writers
- Lack of research
- Accessibility issues with print and other media
- Low circulation
- Lack of trained manpower
- Poor coverage of agricultural news
- Financial constraints

Characteristics of Journalist

- Honest: A trustworthy journalist is one who is honest. Your readers and viewers must trust you, and dishonesty is the surest way to betray that trust.
- Bold: Fortune favors those who take risks, ask uncomfortable questions, and get their hands dirty when the job requires it.

- Courteous: A little courtesy—a "please" or "I'd really appreciate it"—is required if you want people to speak to you about a sensitive subject.
- Compassionate: A journalist should not spend his/her entire career writing only lighthearted pieces. Hard news is difficult to hear because it frequently involves pain or loss. A reporter who understands the human element and empathizes with their subject or source will produce a story that readers will find interesting.He will also realize that he did not harm anyone for the sake of the story.
- Creative: The most memorable stories are those told in a unique and creative manner. The successful journalist does more than simply recount what happened; they craft the story and wield their words like artisanal tools. Most readers and viewers know what to expect from a typical story; blink and lean forward in their seats.
- Humble: A journalist may recognize that he is the world's lone voice. He may be pleased to see his name in the byline of each article. At the same time, he should recognize that his name is associated with every word in that article, even if those words turn out to be false or misleading.History of Farm Journalism in India

History of Farm Journalism in India

Year	Publication
1914	Krishi Sudhar(Hindi) –Agra
1928	Zamin Ryot – Nellore (A> P.) – First regional farm journal.
1931	Agriculture and Livestock– by Imperial council of Agril. Research.
1938	Ryot – by Ryot Seva Sangh
1938	Gaon – Bihar government
1946	Krishak Jagat– Nagpur (weekly)
1948	Kheti– ICAR
1953	Seva gram

ICAR Publication	Ministry of Agriculture through Directorate of Extension	Agricultural Universities
Indian Horticulture	Unnat krishi	Kisan Bharti – Pant Nagar
Indian Livestock	Intensive Agriculture	Farm Digest – Pant Nagar
Indian Journal of Animal Science	Home Science	Changi Kheti – PAU, Ludhiana
Indian Farming	Gharn	Krishi-Go-Vidya – GAU, Anand

Krishi Chayanika	Agricultural Extension Review	Apna Patra – Udaipur (Rajasthan)
Kheti	Kurukshetra (Hindi & English) – Dir. of Rural department	Sheti Bhati – Parbhani (MAU)
Phal – Phool		Parvatiya Kheti–Palampur (H. P.)
		Krishi Lok – Kannada
		Haryana kheti – HAU, Hissar
		Krishi Sansar – Bhubaneswar (Odisha)

3

Newspapers and Magazines As A Communication Media

The term "communication media" describes the channels through which data or information is sent and received. These tools or channels for data storage and transmission are known as transmission and storage means in telecommunication.

It is the effective weapon in today's environment that eliminates societal ills and anomalies.

Popular types of communication media

Television: Transmits and receives moving images that can be monochrome (black-and-white) or coloured, with or without accompanying sound. Audio-visual medium of communication

Radio: Uses electromagnetic waves with frequencies lower than visible light to modulate and transmit signals. Modulation in electronics is the process of changing one or more characteristics of the carrier signal, a high frequency periodic waveform, in relation to a modulating signal. The first really mass means of communication, radio rapidly reached millions of people and changed social attitudes, family dynamics, and how individuals interacted with their surroundings.

Print industry: Grasped the new situation and reorganised itself into a regular and formal sector, although print media in most nations began to specialise in particular fields from the beginning of the 19th century. Three categories—magazines, newspapers, and books—define print media.Outdoor media : Comprises billboards, signs, or placards placed inside and outside of commercial buildings, sports stadiums, shops, and buses.

The internet media communication: Largest mass medium for diverse communications in both Internet and mobile networks according to Internet technology. Email and search engines are popular online media outlets.

Newspaper

Definition: A newspaper is a printed publication with folded, unstapled sheets that is typically published daily or weekly and contains news, articles, ads, and letters.

Criteria of a newspaper

Public accessibility: The contents are reasonably accessible to the public, traditionally by the paper being sold or distributed at newsstands, shops, and libraries, since the 1990s, made available over the Internet with online newspaper websites.

Periodicity: These are published on a consistent schedule, usually once a day or once a week. As a result, news outlets can tell readers about breaking news or events as they happen.

Currency: Its information is as current as permitted by the publication schedule. The amount of time needed to create and distribute a print newspaper limits how current it may be.

Universality: Newspaper covers a wide range of subjects, including corporate and political news as well as updates on science, technology, the arts, and entertainment.

Types of newspaper

National Newspaper: Include some news from around the world but concentrate on news from a particular country/ region.

Example: The Sussex Times, South West Mercury

Regional Newspapers: Include some national and international news, but place a strong emphasis on somewhat in-depth local news subjects. typically centred on towns, cities, or clusters of villages.

Example: Bath Chronicle

Local Newspapers: A newspaper that publishes or makes online/offline news and information relevant to a locality, community, or particular local area.

Example: The Daily Express

Tabloid Newspapers: The biggest type of newspaper is a tabloid! Cover all domestic and foreign news, frequently in a sober or official manner.

Example: The Times

Functions of newspapers

- To inform
- To interpret the news
- To provide a service to readers
- To entertain

Major parts of a newspaper

1. **General news:** The most significant local and international news is contained in this. It typically appears on the newspaper's front page. The most significant news item's title is presented in large, strong letters. It's known as a banner headline.
2. **Local and Foreign News Section:** News from the nation's towns and cities is included in a portion of this section. A different section includes international news.
3. **Editorial Page:** Articles referred to as editorials are published in this section. An editorial expresses the editor's or publisher's perspective on a particular topic or situation.
4. **Weather Section:** Wherever you may need to know the weather, it can be found in this section.
5. **Sports Page:** News on domestic and international sporting events can be found on this page. It also includes athletes who are well-known.
6. **Ads Section:** Advertisements that come within the categories of "Help, Wanted," "For Lease or Sale," or "Wanted to Buy" can be found in this area. Personal and legal notices might also be found in this area.
7. **Business and Finance Section**: Businessmen and those with an interest in business can learn about banking, foreign exchange rates, imports and exports, and the costs of premium commodities in this section.
8. **Entertainment Section:** Information regarding television, radio, cinema, and other entertainment-related topics can be found in this area. Additionally, it has games, puzzles, comic books, cartons, and daily horoscopes.
9. **Society Page:** This section includes news about notable celebrities who are attending special events or giving performances somewhere.
10. **Travel and Tourism Section:** This section offers advice on how to have a great trip. It provides information on the things to do in these locations

and guides travellers to beautiful holiday sites. The schedules for ship and aeroplane departures and arrivals can also be found in this section. both domestically and abroad.

11. **Announcement and Obituary Page:** News on the various religious sects' events, such as fellowships, seminars, prayer gatherings, and the like, is provided in this section. The obituary page contains a list of deceased individuals as well as the date and location of their funeral.
12. **Home and Culture Section**: This section offers tips on creating a budget, preparing meals, improving your home, taking care of your plants, and other related topics.
13. **Reader's Opinion:** This section publishes reader feedback, comments, and the like. The publisher of the newspaper receives correspondence from readers. The majority of those publishers reserve at least half of a page for reader letters.

Magazine

Definition: A magazine is a periodical publication which is printed or electronically published. They are often paid for by subscriptions, purchase fees, advertising, or a mix of the three.

The term "magazine" originally referred to a collection or storage area.

Characteristics of magazines

- Popular magazines offer comprehensive overviews of topics, trade publications report on market trends, novel products or procedures and scholarly journals present in-depth analyses of themes and present research findings.
- Non-technical language is used in a magazine aimed at the general population.
- This content includes general interest pieces, feature articles, and interviews.
- They use many interesting and sometimes sensuous photographs to draw the attention of readers.
- In general, magazine articles are concise, simple to read, and may have pictures or drawings.
- When composing the articles for magazines, a particular format or structure isn't always followed.

- It is more engaging to readers because of its appealing aesthetic, captivating cover images, and artwork printed on high-quality paper.
- Numerous eye-catching and colourful advertising can be found in magazines.

Types of Magazines

- **Magazines of general interest:** Cater the need of entire population and have large circulation. Ex- Reader digest
- **News Magazine:** Produced weekly or fortnightly. Articles on situation, politics, Economics, Religon, industry, sports etc are published
- **High Class Magazines:** Aimed at selected audience, appeal to a particular class. These magazines are serious minded periodicals offering high level reporting with emphasis upon literacy, ethical, social, political or scientific problems.
- **Magazine of Men's Interest:** e.g.-sports, love stories, fashion, photos
- **Technical Magazines:** Are for specialized sections of society i.e. engineering, medicine, agriculture etc.
- **The House Magazine/ Journals:** Produced by companies, organizations etc and are distributed free of cost to employees, customers. The purpose behind is to present the products of a company
- **Religious Magazine:** Akhand Gyan Magazine, East & West Series Magazine
- **Film Magazine:** Femina Magazine
- **Sports Magazine:** Cricketer, sports times etc
- **Magazine For Children:** Phool, Taleem

Functions of magazines

- Offers a more long-form writing.
- Published on a regular basis.
- They are meant to be kept longer than the newspapers.

Magazines serve specific functions to society such as:

- **Surveillance:** They focus on specific fields like science, health, agriculture, etc.

- **Correlation :** They achieve this by explaining certain features of the topic to their audience.
- **Entertainment:** They typically have a lot of entertaining material.
- **Marketing goods and services:** When reading a magazine, people frequently spend more time perusing the advertisements than the editorial material.

Major parts of a magazine

1. **Cover:** The magazine's initial page makes it the most significant in certain aspects. It is never too early to begin considering what would make an excellent cover photo. The majority of editors choose an image that relates to a significant feature that will be added to the publication.
2. **Cover pages:** The cover page follow the cover, are often made of the same material as the cover, and are virtually always ads. Advertising will appear on the cover's second page. The second most expensive ad page is this one. The third cover page, which is once more only available to advertisers, is the third most costly ad page in the publication. The most expensive ad page is the final cover page, which appears on the magazine's back.
3. **Table of contents:** The table of contents provides a concise summary of the magazine's structure following numerous advertisement pages. Flipping to the text and quickly locating the item you were looking for is especially helpful when a reader is fascinated by the cover and wants to read more. The table of contents can be created with or without margins, but it's crucial to identify the content parts so that the reader can grasp the page number, the subject's title, and—if you choose—a quick summary of the topic. This section requires careful consideration of typography.
4. **Imprint:** Although some publications place it toward the back, this section of the magazine is typically located at the front of the book. The staff members of the magazine are listed in the imprint, often known as the "masthead." Writing, marketing, sales, advertising, and editors are all important aspects of the publishing company that creates the magazine. This page has a very plain and tidy style. Typically, the logo is positioned at the top of this page.
5. **Letter from the Editor (s):** It is the magazine's opening editorial page. It is an introduction from the editor in chief outlining the topic's substance. It depends on the journalistic voice and style of the publication. It essentially covers the primary subjects, although it could also include some broader views on the subjects this magazine covers. Typically, it is a page and has a picture that has anything to do with the message or the editor (s).

6. **Articles:** This is the magazine's main body is this. Articles can range in length from being very short to being over ten pages long. Short and long articles typically appear when the magazine is structured. A 4-page piece, for instance, may come after a 10-page article instead of another 10-page item. This improves the magazine's rhythm or flow. Although a specific publication style must be adhered to, the designs associated with these pages offer designers the most creative latitude. It is crucial to stress that each article should be clearly distinguishable from the others because if the reader cannot tell where one article finishes and the other begins, he may become confused.
7. **Back of the book:** The remaining articles, news, listings, columns, and horoscopes are found in this section of the magazine. The magazine's tight structure is followed in this section, precisely as it was at the beginning, and the layout is left untouched. Generally speaking, this is where you can locate "classified" adverts. These pages contain groups of smaller adverts that range in size from 1/4 of a page to 1/16 of a page. Depending on the journal's focus, the final page is usually devoted to a columnist, brief article, quick interview, or other loosely structured content.

Principles followed while writing for a newspaper/magazine in Farm Journalism

- **Simple and clear language**
- **Short sentences-** no longer than 20 words or three ideas.
- **Simple sentence-** active voice is more preferable.
- **Explain any new words whenever you use them**

Difference between newspaper and magazine

Basis	**Newspaper**	**Magazine**
Meaning	A newspaper is a printed publication with folded, unstapled sheets that is typically published daily or weekly and contains news, articles, ads, and letters.	A magazine is a periodical publication which is printed or electronically published. They are often paid for by subscriptions, purchase fees, advertising, or a mix of the three.
Readers	Broad reader base	Limited reader
Publication frequency	Daily, fortnightly, weekly, monthly, quarterly, bi-annually, or annually.	Periodically
Length of the articles	Short and precise	Long and detailed
Price	Economical	Expensive

4

Agricultural Stories

Types

- News story
- Feature story
- Success story
- Popular article
- Radio and TV script
- Process or utility feature
- General information feature
- Experience feature
- Personality feature

News story

- Any new information, idea, event, situation or development, that is of interest to a large number of people, is a news.
- Any event when reported becomes a news.

Types of news

Hard news: Usually relates to issues, politics, economics, global relations, welfare, and science advancements.

Soft news : Centers on celebrities and human-interest stories.

Characteristics of a news

1. **Accuracy:** There should be factual accuracy in a news/ news story.
2. **Objectivity:** A news item ought to be provided objectively and without bias. The full scope of unbiased and brutally honest observation must be shown while presenting news. Due to the fact that people base their ideas on news stories, objectivity is crucial if we want to give consumers confidence. It is much more crucial that it be impartial in every way.

3. **Balanced:** News should be fair in its use of compliments and emphasis. Every aspect of the narrative must be described in minute detail by the reporter. A reporter must carefully choose and organise the information in order to present a fair picture of the entire issue.
4. **Concise:** News must be coherent, succinct, understandable, and simple. A tale that lacks focus, structure, and clarity does not possess the essential elements of news. It must be well-paced, cohesive, and most importantly, written in such a way that the story's purpose is crystal clear.
5. **Current:** If time is not a crucial factor, the definition of news remains incomplete. The news' essential component is time. The emphasis on time in the narrative is essential due to the possibility of change during the transitory era. Most headlines for news items read "today" or, at the furthest, "last night." The news media are quite particular about timing. They assure the audience that the information is not only current but also the final word on the matter.
6. **Nearness:** The closure the information to the receiver geographically and psychologically, the greater is the news value.
7. **Consequence:** The more the audience are affected by the news, the more is its value.

Elements of news

a) **Heading:** The #1 news story is about a capsule opening. The headline must include a summary of all the news that is compelling. It ought to be succinct, unambiguous, and motivating. To make it memorable and catchy, powerful phrases should be used.

b) **Lead:** A news story's offer, or introduction, is its first few sentences. The news is compressed and provides a summary of all the details.

The two primary types of news lead are as follows:

i) Summary lead: As the name implies, a lead composed in this format summarizes its content. The following six questions should be addressed as much as feasible in a summary lead:

- Who?
- What?
- When?
- Where?
- Why?
- How?

ii) **Suspended interest lead:** In a tale known as a suspended interest story, it can be effective and exciting to place the true climax or feature elsewhere other than in the lead. What is referred to as the suspended interest narrative is frequently the most exciting and effective. The closing paragraph of a story frequently contains the climax.

c) **Body:** It provides specific details about the incident. It should be easy to comprehend, simple, and clear.

Forms of news writing

a) **Inverted pyramid pattern:** It is common to represent the structure of the news story, with lead or the summary or the most important facts forming the base, at the top, and the more important detail in one or two paragraphs, followed by more detail and additional facts supporting the main news. The supporting details and information to the main story. the insignificant information and unimportant details from the news story's peak.

Diagrammatic representation of this is as follows:

(Pyramid Structure of News Writing)

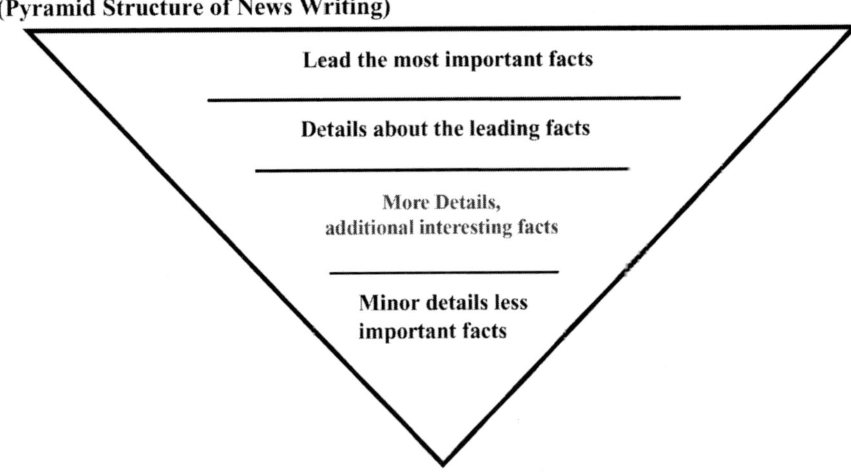

b) **Chronological form:** This format can be used to present a sequence of occurrences chronologically. if you want the reader to quickly understand the order of the events.

c) **Suspended interest form:** When writing a tale, you can occasionally play on the reader's feelings of suspense. Instead of introducing the story's conclusion right away, you make the reader search for it later on in the narrative.

Principles of writing a news story

- The purpose of writing should be clear and specific.
- Know about the people for whom you are writing.
- Know the subject
- Do proper investigation before writing.
- Simple and clear writing should be there.
- Avoid unusual words.
- Do not exaggerate.
- Follow one sentence one idea approach.
- Use appropriate visuals.

Feature story

A feature story typically shows newsworthy events and information through a narrative story with a plot and story characters, as opposed to straight news reporting.

These narratives emphasize emotions and sentiments rather than fundamental truths. These are frequently historical tales of specific individuals.

Characteristics

- Feature stories typically have a powerful narrative line and are highly descriptive and detailed.
- Strong leads in feature tales draw readers in and compel them to keep reading.
- Interviews are frequently used in feature articles.
- Quotes from the subject(s) of feature articles are included.
- Facts and opinions are combined in feature stories, with an emphasis on the human interest aspect of the narrative.
- Feature stories both educate and entertain.

Instructions to write a feature story

- Explore a current issue/topic
- Follows narratorial rules (i.e. There is a plot, complication, and conclusion)
- Write in concise lines.
- Facts and views should be combined.

- Give your take on the subject or problem.
- Include catchy elements.

Success story

Success story is a narrative about someone/ some organisation who achieves fame, renown, or great achievement.

Need of writing

- To educate and influence people.
- To educate stakeholders.
- To gain visibility and credibility.
- For more support and resources.
- To gain popularity.

SRRE of a success story

- Situation: What promoted the programme
- Response: Response of the agency/ individual
- Result: The final outcome
- Evidence: What the evidence and how you evaluate.

Outline of a success story writing

- Title
- Define the problem
- Programme description
- Impact statement
- Contact information

Tips for writing

- Know your story as well as the audience.
- Present a memorable fact.
- Always show benefit.
- Provide credible information.
- Be systematic and consistent.
- Use illustrations.

Popular article

Popular articles are ones that are printed in widely read daily newspapers and other agricultural periodicals and are aimed at farmers and the general public.

Radio script

Radio is a mass communication tool that can inform, pique interest, foster learning, broaden horizons and mental acuity, dispel prejudices, bring enlightenment and encourage favourable attitudes, pique emotion, guide listeners' interest, and aid them in understanding the significance of new ideas and thoughts.

Parts of the scripts

The first half of the script is intended to pique listeners' interest; a compelling introduction piques interest in the subject matter.

The examination of the current state of affairs and a focus on regional issues could be included in the second section.

In order to gain the listener's trust, the third section might explain the recommended practise and why it is superior to the preceding practise.

The concluding section of the script, which continues with an action, can provide a summary of all the various points.

TV script

Story board format

Sl No.	Rough picture of the shot	Brief description	Time	Nature of shot	Narration commentary	Background music

Process or utility feature

This kind of story demonstrates "how to do" a specific, tangible task or "how to build" a particular object that will be useful around the house or on the farm.

Giving the reader step-by-step instructions for carrying out a beneficial process or for creating a useful construction is your major goal when writing a process story.

General information feature

The goal of this type of feature is to "tell" the reader about an issue that is relevant to and interesting to him on a daily basis, as well as how it is to be solved. Such tales can assist him in bettering his way of life, enhancing his farming success, and carrying out daily tasks more effectively by encouraging him to attempt and imitate others' actions.

Experience feature

The experience feature, which makes strong use of human interest, is another type frequently employed by farm and home writers and well-liked by readers.

Personality feature

This type of feature focuses solely on "describing" one specific individual. This narrative is intended to amuse and motivate readers as it discusses the strong character of a person well-known for his accomplishments. Always, a fascinating individual is the subject of this. He must have something noteworthy, interesting, or original to say about life to his credit. In this instance, the focus is far more on the individual than it is on his job or accomplishments.

5

Gathering Information

Sources of information

News is constantly occurring. There is a newsworthy event happening somewhere in the world every minute of every day.

People, letters, books, files, videos, cassettes, and other materials that journalists utilise to put together news articles can all serve as sources of information.

Types of sources

Primary sources: A person with first-hand knowledge of a problem or a document they produced can both be considered primary sources.

They are typically the best sources of knowledge regarding their particular aspect of what occurred. They should be able to provide you with reliable information as well as powerful opinions.

Example: Artifacts, audio recordings, diaries, internet communication, interview, letters, peer-reviewed journal articles, original documents, patents, photos, proceedings, records of organizations, speeches, videos, survey results, works of art, web sites.

Secondary sources: Secondary sources are those who relay the news rather than creating it. Secondary sources include things like an incident's official police report or press officer comments. Primary sources are typically more trustworthy than secondary sources.

Example: Bibliographies, biographies, criticisms, commentaries, dictionaries, encyclopaedias, histories, journal articles, monographs (except fiction and autobiographies), textbooks, websites.

Written sources: A journalist can get a lot of information through written reports. They are normally published with official approval, have undergone extensive investigation by the authors, and have been accuracy-checked.

Reporters: Other journalists are among the most trustworthy (albeit not entirely trustworthy) sources of information. They can be co-workers or journalists from a news source that works with other company. Their reports will typically be accurate and dependable if they are well-trained, experienced, and objective.

Tip-offs: These are the most perilous information sources, so these should be utilised at own risk. On rare occasions, a caller will offer a tip for a story without offering their name. They are allegedly anonymous (meaning "no name").

Press release: Press releases are typically used to announce certain news. The press release includes content that is valuable and has some news value. A press release covers all facets of a certain issue and provides readers with relevant facts and information.

Handouts: The handouts include a wide range of topics, including the regular activities of the ministry or departments, VIP addresses, question and answers in the legislature or in front of the House of Representatives, and the developmental initiatives of government agencies. It includes the department's name for information. If the minister or a government representative spoke in his or her own capacity, no official handout was given.

News Agency

News agencies have been a mainstay of contemporary journalism since they are essential to the gathering, creation, and dissemination of news information to audiences worldwide. By offering in-depth investigative reporting, analysis of political, social, and economic trends, and sometimes coverage of breaking news events, these organisations act as a bridge between media outlets and news sources.

As markets, technology, and social circumstances have changed over time, news organisations have also changed to meet the shifting demands of the public and the media business. They now work for a wide variety of news organisations like multinational news organisations like Reuters and Agence France-Presse including local journalism that serves particular communities.

Functions of News Agency

A news agency's primary duty is to deliver reliable and timely news coverage, with a special emphasis on breaking stories, politics, business, sports, and entertainment. Other than this, the following are some of the main duties of both private and sarkari news outlets.

- Gathering news from many outlets, including news wires, journalists, and correspondents.

- Correcting and confirming news for fairness and accuracy.
- Delivers a wide range of information quickly and effectively.
- Keep up news archives that are a great resource for historians, journalists, and scholars.
- Additionally, produce multimedia material to increase audience accessibility and engagement with news.

News Agencies of India

The public and media industry in India are served by a number of news agencies that cover news. The list of Indian news agencies along with the year of establishment is shown below.

News Agencies	Year of establishment	Place
Press Trust of India (PTI)	1947	New Delhi
United News of India (UNI)	1961	New Delhi
Indo-Asian News Service (IANS)	1986	New Delhi
Asian News International (ANI)	1971	New Delhi
Hindustan Samachar	1948	New Delhi

Press Trust of India

The oldest and biggest news agency in India was founded in 1947 and is called PTI. It has a nationwide network of reporters and offices and offers news services and coverage in both Hindi and English.

- The PTI service is available to readers of over 200 Indian newspapers, including Doordarshan and the government.
- This new agency covers a variety of global cities, including the UK, Africa, Russia, Colombo, and the USA.
- It offers a broad variety of television networks and employs several journalists throughout the globe.
- The PTI has received several honours for its journalism, including the International News Services Award and the Ramnath Goenka Excellence in Journalism Award.
- The Board of Directors oversees the PTI and the current Chairman is K.N. Shanth Kumar, an expert media professional.

United News of India

UNI, a prominent news organisation in India, was founded in 1961. UNI, which is supported by eight national daily, is present in many Indian cities and provides news coverage in Hindi, English, and other languages.

- To deliver worldwide news on your TV, this news organisation has collaborated with several foreign news organisations in the USA, Germany, Italy, and other countries.
- To address the unique demands of its subscribers, UNI has also launched several fantastic projects, such as the Agricultural Service and the Economic Services.
- A wide spectrum of readers, media outlets, and other stakeholders trust UNI's news material because it is recognized for its objectivity and accuracy.
- News content from UNI is also supplied to print, electronic, and digital media outlets in India and beyond.
- UNI has area offices spread around the nation's major cities, with its headquarters being in New Delhi, India.

Asian News International

ANI is one of India's top news agencies and was founded in 1971. has a network of bureaus and correspondents around India and offers news in both Hindi and English. Additionally, ANI was the first news organisation in India to offer syndicated video news.

- ANI has a long history of calling out misreporting media, fake news networks, and government propaganda.
- A wide range of subjects are covered by ANI, including business, politics, sports, entertainment, technology, and both domestic and foreign news.
- For its excellent news coverage, ANI has received several honours and accolades, including the Indian Television Academy Award for Best News Coverage.
- It is a part of the global network of significant news organisations known as International News Services.
- News from ANI is available in English, Bengali, Telugu, Tamil, Hindi, Punjabi, English, and Marathi.

Indo-Asian News Service

It is an Indian private news agency that was founded in 1986. IANS offers news in both Hindi and English and is present in many Indian towns. It also covers worldwide news with the assistance of global network journalists.

- IANS, a preeminent news organisation, is crucial in influencing public perception and raising awareness of many matters of both domestic and global significance.
- A number of media entities, including newspapers, television networks, and digital media platforms, get news content from IANS. In addition, it provides analysis, picture and video content, and real-time news updates.
- Newspapers, television networks, news agencies, and digital media platforms are among the clientele of this Indian news agency, both domestically and internationally.
- It covers news and events from India and across the world, with a focus on technology, business, politics, entertainment, and sports.
- The Press Council of India's National Award for Excellence in Journalism is among the many accolades that IANS has received for its journalism.

Hindustan Samachar

Hindustan Samachar, a well-known news organisation in India, was founded in 1948. It provides services and news coverage in Hindi and English, and it has a nationwide network of offices.

- As a regional news source, Hindustan Samachar covers stories and topics that national news sources might not cover as extensively.
- Hindustan Samachar focuses on sports, politics, business, entertainment, and social concerns while covering news and events from India and throughout the world.
- It has a significant online presence thanks to the news items it posts on Facebook, Twitter, and its own website.
- Hindustan Samachar asserts that its news reporting adheres to strong editorial independence and neutrality, with the values of impartiality, truthfulness, and fairness serving as guiding principles.

News Agencies of World

Around the world, there are several varieties of international news organisations covering anything from political parties to fresh content centered on financial markets. These news organisations have a significant influence on people's lives, both directly and indirectly. The top news organisations in the world are listed below, along with their nation.

News Agencies	Year of establishment	Place
Associated Press	1846	United States
Reuters	1851	United Kingdom
TASS	1902	Russia
BERNAMA	1967	Malaysia
ITIM	1949	Thailand
Agence France-Presse	1835	France
XINHUA	1931	China
KYODO	1945	Japan
ANTARA	1937	Indonesia
Islamic Republic News Agency	1934	Iran
Deutsche Presse-Agentur	1949	Germany
WAFA	1972	Palestine
Australian Associated Press	1935	Australia
NOVOSTI	1918	Russia
Middle East News Agency	1955	Egypt
United Press International	1907	USA

Associated Press

It is one of the world's oldest news agencies, having been established in 1846. Global news, including breaking news, politics, sports, entertainment, and business, is covered by this press.

- News organisations that are members of the AP have access to its materials, which they may utilize to enhance their reporting.
- It is among the most reputable and trustworthy news outlets in the entire globe.
- The Associated Press has more than 2,000 correspondents spread across more than 250 sites globally, providing global news coverage.
- The goal of this global news organisation is to provide people throughout the world with fast, accurate, and unbiased news. The Associated Press has received several honors for its work including many Pulitzer Prizes.

Reuters

It delivers global news with a primary emphasis on business and financial news. Reuters is a British news agency based in the United Kingdom, founded in 1851. The Thomson Reuters Company owns it, and it gives news to businesses, organisations, and media outlets.

- Reuters has more than 2,500 journalists and 600 photographers spread across more than 200 sites globally. The news organisation has received several prizes for its reporting, including 30 Pulitzer Prizes. And it was founded in 1851 in London by industrialist Paul Reuter, a native of Germany.
- Among the most well-known breaking news are the announcement of the armistice that marked the end of World War I, the first images of the aftermath of the 2004 tsunami in the Indian Ocean, and the initial reports of Osama bin Laden's death.
- It covers various aspects of news including sports, business, finance and politics.

Agence France-Presse

AFP is a French news organisation that offers news coverage in a number of languages. It was founded in 1835. It objectively covers a wide range of subjects in business, politics, sports, and entertainment.

- The AFP is a nonprofit organisation that receives funding from the government of France.
- It is renowned for providing in-depth coverage of all happenings in France and its past colonies. It is also well-known for its coverage of conflicts, crises, and significant global events, including the Arab Spring, the European refugee crisis, and the wars in Syria and Iraq.
- The AFP is available in six languages: English, German, French, Spanish, Arabic, and Portuguese.
- With more than 200 bureaus spread over 150 countries, it is among the biggest news organisations globally.

List of some institutions providing information about agriculture

International level

Agricultural Research Information System (AGRIS)

AGRICOLA (Agriculture Online Access)

AGROVOC Thesaurus

Consultative Group of International Agricultural Research (CGIAR)

Commonwealth Agricultural Bureau International (CABI)

National level

Agricultural Libraries

Initiatives in Capacity Building of Agricultural Resources

Agricultural Research Information Centre (AGRIC)

Agricultural Research Information System (ARIS)

Agricultural Research Information System Network (ARISNET)

Consortium of Resources in Agriculture (CeRA)

Krishiprabha

ICT initiatives to meet the information need of farmers

Almost All Questions Answered (aAQUA)

Digital Green-Participatory Video for Agricultural Extension

e-Arik (e-Agriculture) of Arunachal Pradesh

e-Sagu (e- Cultivation)

VILLAGE KNOWLEDGE CENTRES

MSSRF- Village Knowledge Centres (VKCs)

ISRO- Village Resource Centres (VRCs)

Warana wired Village Project

WEB PORTALS

AGRISNET

DACNET

iKisan

Agriwatch Portal

ICT for Market Information And Agri. Business

Agmarknet

ITC-e-Choupal

Farmer Call Centres

SMS Broadcast service by KVK

Interview techniques

An interview is a structured conversation in which one party asks questions and the other responds. In common parlance, a "interview" is a one-on-one conversation between an interviewer and an interviewee.

Principles of interviewing

Empathize, develop discrepancy, deal with resistance, and promote self-efficacy.

How to conduct an interview

Prepare by conducting preliminary research on the subject. - Understanding the fundamentals of a subject is a great place to start when interviewing experts in that field. In-depth research using previous articles, online resources, or existing media aids in developing insight into a specific topic.

Choose an interview format

Interviews can be conducted in a variety of formats and styles, which may influence which questions you ask and how you ask them. Understanding the interview's target audience and considering the best format can help you decide on the interview style and questions to ask.

Set a time, date, and location

The next step is to set a date, time, and location for your interview.

Begin by asking some basic questions

Beginning with simple questions is the best way to make interviewees feel at ease.

Listen intently and ask pertinent questions

Listening to what your source says is important for gathering information and adapting your interview technique with relevant questions and segues.

Concentrate the conversation on your source

Because interviews are conversations, it is critical to relate to and empathize with the interviewee. Interviews, in contrast to everyday conversations, are more one-sided, with the source speaking more about their experience and the journalist prompting. Making sure you're not talking about yourself more than necessary to relate to the interviewee can help you save time and focus on the important information you need.

Finish your interview on time

Respecting your source's and anyone else's time is critical to conducting a successful interview.

Maintain contact and follow up

Following up with your source and staying in touch helps to build a good relationship and opens the door to future interviews.

Tips

Before interview

1. Get to know the person you're going to interview first. Discover who he is, what his name is, what his work entails, and what his accomplishments are.
2. Determine what information you want to glean from the interview.
3. Set up a meeting place, time, and date with him to interview him.
4. Make a list of the key questions you want to ask him in order to obtain the information you require.
5. The question should extract information piece by piece without confusing the interviewer.

During Interview

1. Avoid asking questions that elicit yes or no answers. Allow him to express himself in his own way. Many interesting things will emerge as a result of this.
2. Never give the impression that you are superior to the interviewee or that you are attempting to dominate him. Speak to him in a friendly tone. As a result, his shyness was removed.
3. Take careful notes during the interview on all important statements and details.
4. As soon as possible, put the people you're interviewing at ease (through honesty or feeling at ease). Demonstrate that you are extremely (extremely) interested in him and his activities. Then you can ask your question. Don't be intimidated by them. Always be courteous and respectful to others.

After Interview

Make a plan for your writing.

- Choose the main points that are unique and intriguing to the readers. Make a note of these.
- Determine what should be kept, what should be removed, and what should be added.
- Determine the language to be used and the lead to be given.

Write an article as soon as possible after the interview, while everything is still fresh in your mind.

Keep the following points in mind as you write.

- Include something interesting here and there to keep the readers' attention.
- Keep your writing as brief as possible.
- Determine the'slant' of the article. The term'slant' refers to the point on which you want to place emphasis. For example, fertilizer application may have yielded positive results. This will make an excellent slant.
- Consider a good lead. Give the article a new perspective.

Types of interview

News interview

It is intended to provide readers with expert commentary and illumination (enlightenment or clarification) on a current news item from people who are directly or indirectly connected with the news item. In the event of an accident, the news reporter attempts to interview as many eyewitnesses as possible in order to prepare his story.

The feature based on interviews with various people would significantly increase public knowledge and understanding of the subject. The interviews with various people will not only illuminate and explain various points, but will also provide a better understanding of the subject by clearing many clouded and perplexing facts.

Group/Symposium interview

The reporter obtains information not only from a few people who are directly related to the event, as in the case of an accident, but also from a number of people who are not directly related to the event.

The interviewees in a symposium interview are chosen not for their authority on the subject or topic, but as ordinary citizens whose opinions are worth reporting. There are no hard and fast rules about how thoroughly the survey was carried out. Furthermore, different respondents should be asked the same question in substantially the same words and manner.

Personality interview

It is done to reveal a person's personality who is being interviewed. It is not the same as a biographical sketch. The biography includes information such as when the person was born, how many children he had, when he became ambassador, and so on. Biography is useful in writing obituaries, but it rarely brings out a person's qualities and lacks warmth and intimacy (familiarity).

In a personality interview, the interviewer chooses a man or woman who is either a newsworthy personality or has become newsworthy due to certain personality traits - eccentricity, oddity of habit, or circumstances.

Covering Agricultural Events

Types of events

Meetings

Under state or federal law, the majority of public bodies' meetings are open to the public. Understand the relevant laws so that you can ask why a meeting was called to end and provide a valid explanation or point out that the reason was not compliant with your laws. Work sources to find out what transpires in private gatherings

Press conference

A press conference is a formal gathering designed to provide information and address inquiries from the press. Although newsmakers occasionally view press conferences as more effective means of handling the media, journalists typically prefer conducting their own interviews. If you would rather have the answers to questions answered only, don't ask them at a press conference; instead, try to arrange a private interview. Take advantage of the press conference if it's your only chance to have a question answered.

Trials

Find out if live coverage on computers and/or phones is permitted in your jurisdiction. If the judge makes that choice, ask them early enough so you can arrange your coverage (or appeal a decision).

Concerts

Make sure your editor or news director knows if you're writing an entertainment review or covering a news event when you're covering a concert or festival. Take into account the audience response and the performance's relative importance in both situations. If there was something you felt was lacking but the audience loved it, you should at least think about mentioning that in addition to your criticism.

Conferences

When reporting on events like speeches, conventions, conferences, and symposia, you must take your audience into account as well as the relative newsworthiness of various sub-events within larger events. Are you covering a single speaker or panel, or should you cover the entire event? If you are unable to attend multiple events at once, you can make up for missed opportunities by using social media to follow the speaker, speaking with attendees, or conducting interviews.

Sporting events

With the increasing importance of live coverage and postgame enterprise, the "game story" is changing in some ways. Even though notes or live coverage follow the action in a play-by-play manner, the significance and result of a game story take precedence over play-by-play. What was the major development in this game? That's what your coverage should be all about.

Debates

Reported facts should not be subordinated to post-debate —spin_. After a debate, no one can tell for sure who "won," but everyone declares victory, so covering the candidates' actual actions and statements should take precedence over their spin.

Tips for covering

Preparation

Find out as much as you can about the event's schedule in the lead-up. There may be a program or roster with the names and numbers of the players at a sporting event. A public gathering may have a schedule. The speakers will be listed in the conference program. An organizer who can give an overview and some background will be present at a less formal program.

But there are instances when you have to go beyond the organizers and the handouts. Locate some dissenters who can inform you of any fascinating detours the event may take.

Make thorough notes

Using initials or other abbreviations for people is a useful note-taking method for events. For example, you may recognize me as —JM— if I'm speaking at the event.

However, check the schedule to make sure I'm the only one speaking with those initials.

For the most part, your tweets or blog posts can serve as your notes if you're live tweeting or blogging. However, for actual notes, always have a notebook on hand (or perhaps a Word document on your laptop or tablet): information you should confirm before publishing, topics to discuss in interviews during a pause or following the event, and potential follow-up ideas.

Get a 360-degree perspective

In any case, the audience may offer some possible narratives, occasionally a more compelling one more so than the keynote speaker or another main attraction. During an event, the renowned Canadian writing coach Don Gibb advocates for taking a 360-degree perspective, which involves looking both behind and around oneself instead of merely staring at the speaker.

Await the unexpected

Most things go according to plan. On the other hand, surprises do occur. Stay vigilant and modify your plans in case of unforeseen events.

Visual material

Visual material must be included in event coverage. If you're not working with a visual journalist, you must arrange to supply the images and/or videos required for your coverage.

Take pictures of the audience and the speaker(s). Unless you are trying to capture a crowded room, avoid shooting from the back of the room. Approach the speaker closely enough to get a good picture of them.

A video story summarizing the event or a video highlight or highlights to accompany a text story can be used as video coverage, as can a live stream via Periscope, Facebook Live, Livestream, or another live video service.

Write

Even if you don't have an urgent deadline, the sooner you can write after an event, the more accurate and fresh your story will be. You can write more quickly and accurately after the event if you can write a few paragraphs during a break before you decide on your lead or final story.

Provide an answer to the query, "What's this story about?" This should help you determine the main idea of your narrative and aid in developing your lead.

Follow-Up

A meeting story is frequently not as significant as the enterprise story that follows when describing the results of a board or council decision. After an event that has significance for your community, find out what people thought.

Fact-check the remarks made by politicians during speeches or debates. Good enterprise stories can be found in reports and other documents that are distributed, approved, or handled on a regular basis in meetings, especially for beat reporters. Feature stories and sports enterprises frequently stem from in-game events: an examination of a faltering offense or defense, or a feature on a rising star.

Social networks

Observe social media before, during, and after an event. For your story, you may compile a few quotes from readers' reactions, add a few embeds, or select comments for a sidebar. Social media may pose queries that you should investigate further for your reporting.

Wire Services

- A wire service, known as a news agency, a news cooperative, or a news service, distributes news reports to media outlets by wire.
- It is an organisation that compiles news stories and sells them to news organisations that subscribe to its content, like newspapers, magazines, radio stations, and television broadcasters.
- Hard-news articles, features, and other content are created by wire services with little to no editing for usage by media outlets. Additionally, some wire services send images, infographics, and broadcast reports.
- The service charges for the use of its content. Some additionally charge for extras. The wire service takes various forms. While news outlet cooperatives share their material with other members, corporate models may only sell their service.
- Government-operated, non-profit, and alternative media networks are other forms of wire services.

Abstracting

- Abstracting is the process of taking away or removing characteristics from something in order to reduce it to a set of essential characteristics.
- An abstract should essentially be a condensed version of all the sections of a research paper. To put it another way, someone who merely reads the abstract should be able to understand the study's purpose, methodology, key findings, and significance.

6

Headline and Title Writing

- A title should be able to talk. It ought to make a point that both informs and amuses the audience.
- A headline needs to be concise and sum up the story.
- A headline should engage readers and entice them to read the material behind it.
- Make use of recognisable acronyms.
- Assist in setting the publication's general tone.
- The headline ought to be assertive and upbeat.
- Function as a visual component on the page.

Choosing and designing news headlines

- If necessary, the headline should be written in all capital letters.
- Double-tick the letter that needs to be capitalised.
- The catch line is placed in the top right-hand corner, with the edition and page mark in the top left-hand corner.
- Additionally, it contains directions for the headline style, type, and columns that the title will be stretched throughout.
- If the default headline style is set to left in that scenario, the instructions are not necessary.
- The style-breaking headlines must, however, be identified using words and symbols.

Kicker

A one-line heading with a second line (Kicker) above it in a different style and with half the type size makes up the kicker, another typical headline. Only halfway above the main line does it extend (Bush, 1970).

- Kicker headlines are used to provide diversity and spice up a page. A kicker headline is a brief line of display type that is positioned above the main part of the headline and is often no larger than half the point size of the main headline. The kicker is also known as the eyebrow or tagline on some papers (Eisentein, 1983).

- A line of type that appears directly above the main headline is called a kicker. The objective is to rapidly summarise some noteworthy aspects of the narrative below, as well as supplementary information in the main head below (Baskette F. K., 1982).

Hammer

The inverse of the kicker is the hammer, which is typically written in all capital letters. The primary headline is in smaller type, and the big type is the kicker. The hammer can be expressed with no more than one or two words. Hammers make a strong impression on readers due of their size. However, if there are too many hammers on a page, it may lose its impact and lose its aesthetic appeal (Arnold E. G., 1969).

Vertical headlines

The text runs in a single column, and vertical headings are positioned within the basic single-column grid's width (Baskette, F. K., 1982). The range of news value expression in this earliest format is constrained. A maximum of stories can be provided above the fold, despite the grim visuals (Flesh, 1974).

Horizontal headlines

Another headline design with more emphasis potential is this one. It is modular, with the text squared under the headers of multiple columns to form a horizontal unit.

These components are then arranged flat on top of one another to create the page. A lengthy story appears shorter in this style. Without needing to shuffle the paper up and down, complete stories can be read with the page folded at the natural mid-page fold. Because headlines are separated from one another by text, each title retains its impact. With a horizontal layout, the entire width of the page can be displayed. However, just a few storeys above the midfield are visible from retail establishments.

The distinctive feature of a horizontal makeup is that stories are carried into three or more neighbouring columns and have a horizontal shape. Despite the fact that a tale may be prolonged into the next adjacent column, this does not always result in a horizontal makeup because the story's shape may instead be vertical.

Stories are squared off at the bottom, which is another characteristic of horizontal makeup. This indicates that each column where the story is continued has the same depth.

Banner headline

The initial headlines consisted of just one column. They can now fill the newspaper column in its entirety. Depending on the significance of the story, newspapers today blend single column and multi-column headlines for display.

Lower case letters across such a vast measure look straggly, therefore the banner headline shouldn't be written in them. Additionally, headlines must be concise; else, they risk being overly wordy.

Flush left

One or more of the lines in the flush left heading are offset to the left. The column rule shouldn't be affected by this. A two or three line headline with each line flush left is referred to as a flush left headline. The width and setting of the lines are not need to be equal.

Flush right

To give the left side of the page a stepped appearance, each line is pressed up against the right margin. Its usage is considerably more constrained than the stepped headline. Although it might appear on occasion in a newspaper, it cannot be advised as a standard style. It appears to be set and challenging to read.

Drop heads

Drop heads are often referred to as a deck or a dropout headline. A drop head is an additional headline that provides more details and appears below the primary headline. It ought to function as a secondary but relevant headline that can stand alone (Baskette, F. K., 1982).

Centered

Each line of the headline type is centred on the column's white in this layout. Whether it is a multi-line or multi-deck heading, it is well-designed, centred, and cleanly framed in white.

The patterns created by this need slightly more attention than the patterns the flush left heading creates, but neither needs as much attention as some other patterns. If one is writing multi-deck headlines they should be centered where they look best.

The common double column headline is a single deck of two lines with centered headings. The second line should always be shorter than the first at least by two units (Baskette F. K., 1982).

Stepped

In this configuration, the middle lines are centred, the last line is flush right, and the first line is flush left. The lines should be around the same length and resemble steps. A smooth step necessitates meticulous headline drafting. The current readability experts discourage this style. The stepped style's greatest challenge, however, is that it relies too heavily on accurate counting, and any errors might produce unattractive outcomes (Garcia, 1993).

Quotes

One strategy for handling strong opinions in keynote speeches or political party resolutions is to use quotes. The speaker or group's name may be included in the headline. Completely quote-based headlines are typically weak and should never be used. When a headline truly calls for single quotes, it is preferable to utilise them (Entman, R. M. 2004).

The attribution is frequently stated in the second deck when the headline is in decks. It's not a good idea. An attribution in the second deck cannot make a headline with an opinion and no quotes acceptable.

7

Writing Story Organisation and Treatment of Story

Fundamentals of writing farm stories

1. Use of plain and simple language: A farm journalist would have translated technical terms into their plain language.
2. Presentation of novel ideas: People are open to new concepts that are logically explained and will increase their return on investment as a whole.
3. Keep the message brief and to the point so that farmers can recall it. The information should be focused on the benefits that can be attained without using an excessive amount of wording.
4. Use of visuals: Visuals add interest, are more memorable, and have deeper significance. A statement is more understandable and pleasing to the eye when there are more visuals present.
5. Farmers are very receptive to messages that are recent, reliable, realistic, and relevant (the "4Rs").
6. The audience appreciates and accepts the message that is centred on their environment, locations, and selves.

Organisation and treatment of story

Writing a plan

- Make a strategy in writing before you start a story that is likely to be challenging. Whether it's a memo to an editor, a strategy for your own use, or the beginning of a story, get writing.
- Writing will enable you to express yourself clearly and lay out your lines of inquiry. Writing is your finest form of communication.
- What do you hope the tale will ultimately reveal? What location will you use to search for the data? Why should the viewer be interested?

Discuss your plan

- Discuss your strategy with your supervisor. Some reporters wait until they have something to demonstrate before talking plans with editors. However, a plan maker can help you refine it. If your plan overlaps, conflicts, or dovetail with the plans of another writer, an editor may be able to tell. Your strategy can be pursued with the help of an editor.
- Talk about the strategy with your co-workers as well. Talk about it and get advice from a more seasoned journalist who has handled comparable stories in the past.

Inquire about the plot

Focus your reporting

Write as you report

"Outline" your notes

Some writers adhere to them religiously, while others find them unnecessary. Whether you write a formal plan or not, it's helpful to arrange your notes in a loose framework while writing a complex novel.

Look over your notes, documents, and other materials, marking any pertinent information, quotes, or facts with a source or topic label.

8

Readability

The ease with which a text can be read is referred to as readability. Complexity, recognizability, legibility, and typography are all possible inclusions. Sentence length, syllable density, and word familiarity are common considerations in readability algorithms.

It refers to how easily a reader can comprehend a written content. The complexity of a text's vocabulary and syntax, as well as how it is presented, determine how easily it may be understood in natural language (such as typographic aspects like font size, line height, and line length).

Why is readability important?

Readability is more than just legibility, which measures how well a reader can discern between individual letters or characters. For all readers, but especially for those who struggle with reading comprehension, higher readability reduces reading effort and increases reading speed. By raising a text's readability from mediocre to good can make the difference between its communication goals succeeding or failing with readers who have average or poor reading comprehension.

It is significant since it affects how easily a reader can comprehend a piece. We can make a document as clear as possible and better match it with its audience by analysing the readability of the text.

Striving for good readability increases the possibility that the reader will comprehend your thoughts and ideas without any difficulty. Good readability reduces misunderstandings and enables the reader to quickly and efficiently comprehend the knowledge you've presented without investing a lot of effort.

- Researchers have used various factors to measure readability, such as
- Speed of perception
- Perceptibility in peripheral vision
- Visibility
- Reflex blink technique

- Rate of work (reading speed)
- Eye movements
- Fatigue in reading

Popular readability formulas

1. The Flesch formulas

Rudolf Flesch, in his PhD dissertation, *Marks of a Readable Style*, included a readability formula to predict the difficulty of adult reading material in 1943 which was:

Reading Ease score = 206.835 − (1.015 × ASL) − (84.6 × ASW)

Where: ASL = average sentence length (number of words divided by number of sentences)

ASW = average word length in syllables (number of syllables divided by number of words)

- Publishers found that using the Flesch formulas might boost readership by up to 60%. The work of Flesch had a significant influence on journalism as well.
- The Flesch Reading Ease formula evolved into one of the most popular, validated, and trustworthy readability metrics.
- In 1951, Farr, Jenkins, and Patterson simplified the formula further by changing the syllable count. The modified formula is:
- **New reading ease score = 1.599 nosw − 1.015sl − 31.517**

  Where: nosw = number of one-syllable words per 100 words and

  sl = average sentence length in words.
- The new formula is now called the Flesch–Kincaid grade-level formula.

2. The Dale–Chall formula

- One of the first to criticise Thorndike's vocabulary-frequency lists was Edgar Dale, an education professor at Ohio State University. He argued that they failed to differentiate between the various connotations that many words have.
- Two additional lists of his own were made by him. Irving Lorge utilised a list of 769 simple words as his "short list" in his formula. The other was his "long list" of 3,000 simple terms, which 80% of fourth-graders could understand.

- But, the word lists must be expanded to include common noun plurals, common past tense verb forms, common progressive verb forms, etc. He combined this list with a formula he created with Jeanne S. Chall in 1948, who would go on to found the Harvard Reading Laboratory.

For application of the formula:

1. Pick out a few 100 word samples scattered across the book.
2. Calculate the average word count each sentence (divide the number of words by the number of sentences).
3. Determine the percentage of terms that are NOT included in the Dale-Chall list of 3,000 simple words.

Raw score = 0.1579*(PDW) + 0.0496*(ASL) if the percentage of PDW is less than 5 %, otherwise compute Raw score = 0.1579* (PDW) + 0.0496* (ASL) + 3.6365

Where: Raw score = uncorrected reading grade of a student who can answer one-half of the test questions on a passage.

PDW = Percentage of difficult words not on the Dale–Chall word list.

ASL = Average sentence length

Finally, to compensate for the "grade-equivalent curve," apply the following chart for the final Score

Raw score	**Final score**
4.9 and below	Grade 4 and below
5.0–5.9	Grades 5–6
6.0–6.9	Grades 7–8
7.0–7.9	Grades 9–10
8.0–8.9	Grades 11–12
9.0–9.9	Grades 13–15 (college)
10 and above	Grades 16 and above

3. The Gunning fog formula

Robert Gunning contributed to the introduction of readability research to the workplace in the 1940s. He established the first readability consultancy company in 1944 with the goal of clearing out the "fog" in corporate writing and media. He released The Art of Clear Writing in 1952 using his own Fog Index formula, which has a correlation of 0.91 with reading comprehension as determined by testing.

The formula is one of the most reliable and simplest to apply:

Grade level= 0.4 * ((average sentence length) + (percentage of Hard Words))

Where: Hard Words = words with more than two syllables.

Readability and newspaper readership:

- Wilber Schramm conducted one interview with 1,00 newspaper readers and he discovered that the amount of reading an article receives is influenced by the reading style. This was referred to as reading depth, perseverance, or persistence. He also discovered that readers prefer shorter articles and will read less lengthy ones. Three out of ten readers will stop reading a tale after the fifth paragraph if it has nine paragraphs. It will only lose two in a shorter story. Moreover, Schramm discovered that using subheads, bolded paragraphs, and stars to break up a tale actually discourages people from reading.
- Flesch and Gunning, two readability specialists, worked closely with newspapers to assist them make their content more readable. Newspapers saw a significant rise in circulation even with a slight readability improvement. According to one study, increasing readability resulted in a 93% increase in the overall number of paragraphs read.
    - They split up the text into brief paragraphs for visual readability, making it simple to comprehend. Also, they are aware that pictures enhance the reader's ability to see their narrative visually.
    - They balance the length of their sentences in accordance with the substance. They don't use a lot of short sentences because doing so would make their writers sound robotic, but neither are they unduly long.

9

Illustrating Agricultural Stories

A decoration, interpretation, or visual explanation of a text, concept, or process that is intended to be included in published media including posters, flyers, magazines, books, teaching materials, animations, video games, and films is called an illustration.

Using Illustrations

We can comprehend information better when it is shown. Illustrations were one of our first forms of communication, long before any kind of contemporary writing. In reality, new discoveries of cave drawings from more than 35,000 years ago show that humanity have been using images to communicate for a very long time. This did not occur by accident; according to study, over 90% of the information we process is visual, and a significant portion of our brain is dedicated to visual processing.

Benefits of using Illustrations

- Aid in bridging cultural divides

  Several versions of our text must be written in order to communicate an idea in writing while taking into account the various languages of our readers. By using an illustration, we may explain the same concept to those who do not speak the same language.

- Graphics make our products more enjoyable

  In addition to helping us communicate the concept of our product, engaging illustrations also provide our products content and personality that could otherwise be lacking.

- Stimulate user's imagination

  Your creativity expands with illustrations. Graphics assist our users envision themselves in that scenario and provide just the perfect amount of freedom for interpretation.

Use of Photographs

An audience can rapidly understand your message without having to read a lot of text when you use a picture or image. Images provide a captivating and exciting element to any tale, whether it is published online or in print.

- Photos in journalism can reflect on the past as well as inform, educate, and enlighten readers about current issues. The credibility of the narrative is increased by photographs in newspapers.
- A photograph can be used as a tactic to grab readers' attention and break up the monotony of news information because of its aesthetic qualities. As a result, photos improve and embellish newspaper pages.
- A picture in a newspaper is worth a thousand words. An image can be understood without any academic schooling. As a result, pictures can successfully express a message despite literacy barriers.
- Pictures draw readers' attention: A media release, magazine article, or blog post with an image will draw readers' attention more effectively than one with just a block of text. This might encourage more people to read the accompanying article.
- Pictures tell a story: Sometimes, a picture may express a tale more effectively than words ever could. A reader may relate to a scenario that is extremely emotional, such as a family that has recently come together after a horrific incident, more than they would if it were merely written.
- Graphics may swiftly convey a message: Website articles are frequently skimmed over rather than fully read by website visitors. A image is a fantastic method to get your point across to a crowd without them having to read a lot of words.
- Shareability: As images are simple to distribute, a wider audience will be exposed to your tale. You may even incorporate a link in the image to a the writing you want your target audience to read.

Use of Graphs

A specialised type of journalism known as "graphics journalism" presents information using graphic formats. In general, graphic journalism supports and supplements existing reporting and writing that the publisher has done. In order to create a graphic for the narrative, graphics journalists typically choose one section of a story that lends itself to graphic presentation and conduct extra reporting. Such reporting is quite challenging because it needs to be accurate and comprehensive. Additionally, it must generate data that may be effectively used in a graphic manner.

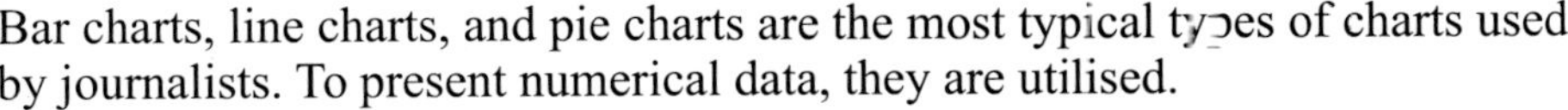

Bar charts, line charts, and pie charts are the most typical types of charts used by journalists. To present numerical data, they are utilised.

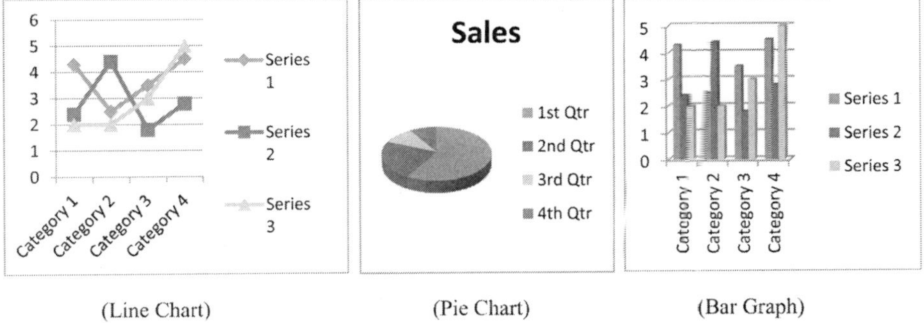

(Line Chart) (Pie Chart) (Bar Graph)

The use of these many types of charts is subject to specific guidelines, which graphics journalists must be aware of and strictly abide by. For instance, a pie chart can only be used to display the components of a whole. There are a few basic rules that needed to be followed are:

- Check the data
- Explain encodings
- Label axes
- Include units
- Keep your geometry in check
- Include your sources
- Consider your audience

Mapping in journalism

Maps are frequently used as graphic elements in publications, and a good one can help the reader understand the setting and location of the events being covered. Integrating all of your reporting is possible with mapping. The reader will likely find a map in a newspaper much more appealing than interminable columns of facts. The reader can better visualize the data thanks to the map.

GIS is used by journalists to examine and depict location-based trends in an expanding body of data. Maps offer crucial context that helps media audiences' better grasp current events. The where and the why are connected by journalists through mapping tales about people and locations.

Reporters can convey patterns to an audience by making straightforward shaded area maps. GIS tools can be used to go farther and unearth unexplored spatial linkages.

10

Caption Writing

Cutlines, another name for photo captions, are a few lines of text that provide context or additional information for published images. In some circumstances, captions and cutlines are distinct from one another. A caption is a brief (often one-line) title or explanation for the picture, whereas a cutline is a longer, prose block that describes the picture more thoroughly, provides context, or connects it to the article.

The first things people read in a publication are frequently the photo captions. A crucial component of a news photographer's job is writing captions for photos. The reader should receive the essential information from a photo caption in order to comprehend the image and its news value.

Caption writing should adhere to the same professional standards of clarity, accuracy, and completeness as any other writing that appears in a publication. A lousy caption can lessen the impact of a beautiful photo and damage the caption's reputation as journalism by being uninformative or, worse, misleading. Why should readers believe the rest of the publication if they can't trust the accuracy of the straightforward information in a caption?

How to Write Good Captions in Photojournalism

One crucial aspect of journalism is captioning images. The information in the captions must be correct. In fact, before deciding whether to read the story itself, most readers prefer to first glance at the images and then the subtitles in a piece of writing. To write a caption that will pique the reader's interest enough to make them read the tale, consider the following ideas.

Learning Caption Basics

1. Verify your facts, first

Accuracy is one of the most crucial components of any kind of journalism. Use of inaccurate information tarnishes the trustworthiness of the article or image. Be sure all information in any captions for photos is accurate before uploading or printing them.

If you are having problems checking your facts—either because you can't find the right source or because you have a deadline—don't print an inaccurate caption. If you are unsure of the accuracy of the material, it is preferable to leave it out.

2. Describe a not-so-obvious item

A photo caption isn't very useful if it just lists the image's elements. If you have a photo of a sunset and just caption is as "a sunset" you're not offering any further information for the reader. Instead, describe non-obvious aspects of the image, such as the setting, the season, the day of the week, or an ongoing event.

- As an illustration, you could want to caption a picture of a sunset as "Pacific coast sunset, March 2016, from Long Beach, Vancouver Island."
- Steer clear of expressions such as "is seen," "is portrayed," "and looks on," and "above."

3. Avoid beginning a caption with specific terms

A caption shouldn't start with "a," "an," or "the." These terms are overly simple and, when unnecessary, take up valuable captioning space. For example, instead of saying: "A blue jet in the boreal forest;" simply say: "Blue jet flying through boreal forest."

- Also, avoid beginning a caption with someone's name; instead, begin the caption with a description before adding the name. For example, don't say: "Modiji near Sunshine Meadow Park." Instead say: "PM Modiji near Sunshine Meadow Park."
- In order to pinpoint a person's location in a picture, you can say "from left." you do not have to mention "from left to right."

4. Name the major people in the shot

If your photo features prominent people, identify who they are. If you know their names, include them (unless they've asked to remain anonymous). If you don't know their names, you might want to write something like "protesters on the streets of Janata maidan" in their place.

- Although it shouldn't be necessary to mention it, be sure that the spelling and title of any and all names you use are accurate.

- You do not have to mention each person in the photo's caption if they are part of a group or if their presence is not necessary to the narrative (i.e., their names are not necessary to convey the narrative).

5. Be as detailed as you can

This advice and accuracy go hand in hand. Find out if you aren't sure who is in the picture or where it was taken. Displaying a picture without providing any context cannot be helpful to the reader, especially if you are unable to explain where the picture was taken.

- If you were collaborating with another journalist for the story, contact them for extra information if needed.
- Identifying where a certain individual is in the picture might be quite helpful if you're trying to identify them. For example, if Kumar is the only one in a hat, you can say: "Kumar, back row in hat."

6. Label historical photos accurately

Make sure the photo is correctly labeled and contains the date (or at least the year) it was shot if you plan to include it in your tale. You might also have to provide attribution to additional photographers and/or organizations, depending on who owns the image.

7. Use present tense in captions

Use the present tense in your captions because most news article images depict events that are now occurring. Any historical photographs would be the obvious exception, as doing so makes sense. The wonderful thing about choosing the present tense is that it provides a sense of immediacy and improves the effect of the photo on the reader.

8. When a photo isn't meant to be hilarious, stay away from humour

Don't attempt to be humorous in the caption if the picture you're captioning depicts a sombre or serious occasion. Only use humorous captions when the image itself is a joke or depicts a humorous circumstance that will make the reader smile.

9. Always remember to give credit and provide citations

The photographer's name and/or the name of the company that owns the image should appear next to each image. Aperture, film speed, f-stop, lens, and other technical information about how the photo was taken are also included in actual photographic magazines and publications.

Enhancing the Story with Captions

1. Use the caption to tell the reader something new
2. Avoid making judgmental statements
3. Do not worry about length of the caption
4. Write in a conversational language
5. Include unessential story items in the captions
6. Determine what punctuation should be used

Avoiding Caption Mistakes

1. Do not be arrogant
2. Avoid making assumptions
3. Make sure you aren't sloppy
4. Remember that what you print is considered fact

Captions: Captions are the little "headlines" over the "cutlines" (the words describing the photograph).

Cutlines: Cutlines (at newspapers and some magazines) are the words (under the caption, if there is one) describing the photograph or illustration.

11

Editorial Mechanisms

Editing

Editing is the process of refining the content, structure, grammar, and presentation of a written work. Editing is done to make sure that your thoughts are communicated to the reader as clearly as possible.

It takes more than just changing a word, adding a comma here and there, and fixing spelling errors to edit a tale. The procedures below must be followed in order to edit effectively.

1. Read the story from beginning to end first. The writer's intent will become clearer to you at this point. Then check to see if it addresses the following queries: what? Why? Where? When? Who? and how - regarding the topic.
2. Make your notes in the margin while keeping these inquiries in mind.
3. Next, consider the general level of education and comprehension of your magazine or letter's readers. Make a note of every word you believe they won't comprehend.
4. Next, determine how long the story should be. What room in your magazine can you offer it? It is preferable to rewrite the story rather than attempt to condense it by omitting some details if you need a very brief copy.
5. Verify that the information is logically ordered and, if a process story, that the directions are comprehensive and given in the right sequence.
6. Examine the content to see if there is only one point of view or if the reader is confused by a variety.
7. Remove any information that does not contribute to the story's main idea or that hinders the reader's comprehension of it.
8. Remove any extraneous words, phrases, sentences, or even paragraphs.
9. Find methods for "bringing life" to the narrative by creating titles and sub-titles. If the title doesn't suit you, you can change it or replace it with a more appealing one.
10. Take note of the lead. It ought to get right to the point. It ought to meet the requirements of a solid lead.

11. Examine the length of the sentences. Divide lengthy paragraphs into manageable, shorter ones.
12. Review each paragraph. Divide lengthy paragraphs into manageable, shorter ones.
13. Remove any unused, obscure, and pompous technical terms. They have no place in the type of tale you wish to tell your viewers.
14. While making all of these modifications, be sure to adhere as closely as you can to the writer's style.
15. Review it thoroughly. Verify that you have not altered the meanings of the writer's assertions. Check to see whether the revised version is indeed a significantly superior version of the original and not just an altered copy. Editing is only done for that reason.
16. Show it to the author if you can. That will guarantee that the information he provided was not altered or omitted during editing. He will be able to mention any that have been altered or omitted.
17. Define the breadth of the material column that will be assembled.
18. Specify the typefaces and sizes to be used for the text, captions for graphics, sub-titles, and sub-headings.
19. Galley proofs will be sent to you first by the printer. To ensure that no words, sentences, or lines were missing during composition, compare them to the original text. Keep an eye out for the names and numbers.
20. Don't make any significant adjustments or edits to the proofs. You will be charged for recomposing such additions or substitutions.
21. Make all edits in the margin after proofreading... Never edit in the middle of a line.

Proof reading

Proofreading is the process of going through a document to look for flaws in spelling, grammar, punctuation, and lack of consistency in text style, including fonts, bold and italic text, spacing, underscore, etc. Copyediting, on the other hand, is a more involved procedure. This includes revising the text to enhance its flow and structure in addition to performing all the necessary proofreading checks.

To prevent errors in printed information, proofreading is done. It is assigned to a person or people to carefully check written material for typos. A proof is essential to proofreading. A proof is just a printed copy of text that has been set in type. Proofreading involves checking the proof for errors.

By using symbols, the proofreader can give instruction without having to explain verbally what needs to be corrected or type out specific instructions. Always remember to draw a line from the error to the margin when proofreading. Put the proofreading symbol at the end of the line. Such symbols are explained below:

Symbol	Example	Meaning
lc	/Farmer	Use a small letter (lower case)
cap	/farmer	Use a capital letter (upper case)
[	child/	Push to left
]	/child	Push to right
][	/child/	Central material
└┘	He was a very strong boy	Push it down
┌┐	He was a very strong boy	Push it up
stet	He was a ~~very~~ strong boy	Let it stand as it was
¶	The farmer came/It is hot	Make a new paragraph
No ¶	The farmer came. /It is hot	No paragraph
tr	The monsoon early arrived	Transposition - words
tr	The monsonos arrived	Transposition - letters or figures
tr	There he bought some fruit Krishna Rao went to the shop	Transposition - lines
(.)	Krishna Rao went to the shop/	Indicates a period
(,)	He had rice, wheat/maize and jowar	Indicates a comma
(;)	He ate rice/it was good	Indicates a semicolon
(:)	They are as follows/	Indicates a colon
“∨	“Stop/ he said	Indicates a quote mark
’∨	The farmer/s crop is good	Indicates apostrophe or single quote
sp.out	ICAR	Spell out : no abbreviation
small/	He was a/boy	Insert word
ℓ	The rice was uncooked	Delete – take out
bf	Fertilizer increases yields	Make it bold face type
#	He went to/the field	Space between words
⌒	Res earch is needed	Close up or join letters
⤷	He became ill. He was dizzy He was struck on the head.	Join material
-	He has a 50/horsepower	Indicates a hyphen
|–|	The tall man/nearly six feet – had a black beard	Indicates a dash

Layout and designing

The area of graphic design known as page layout deals with how visual elements are arranged on a page. To accomplish particular communication goals, organisational composition concepts are typically used. The high-level page layout includes selecting the general text and image placement as well as the medium's size or shape. It necessitates intellect, sentience, and creativity and is influenced by society, psychology, and the message and points of emphasis that the authors and editors of the document want to convey.

Layout is the logical organisation of several visual components of communication, such as a piece, illustration, write-up (text, header, and slogan), colour, and white space, in a way that is pleasing to the eye and facilitates easy and convenient reading.

Principles of layout

1. Proportion

The basis for the relationship between breadth and height is a set of Greek principles. You may have observed that regular shapes like circles and squares draw the eye. They briefly capture our attention. A rectangle has an attractive but more intriguing shape. The Greeks called the 3-by-5-unit rectangle "the Golden Rectangle." They thought the proportion was the most acceptable and aesthetically pleasing. These dimensions are still present on 11X 17 pads and 3X5 cards nowadays. Some of the fundamentally sound ratios are listed below, along with the multiplicative factors for each.

- Long ratio 1:2 (2)
- Golden Rectangle 3:5 (1.62)
- Regular Ratio 4:6 (1.5)
- Hypotenuse Ratio 5:7 (1.41)
- Printer's Ratio 2:3 (1.73)

2. Balance

Perhaps the most crucial layout design rule is balance. The technique of balancing involves grouping visual components of a communication (piece, parts of whole) so they appear to form a single unit or order rather than a variety of independent components. Uneven distribution of the visual components throughout the layout space is highly undesired. Also, it is typically useless to place all the components in a single end or corner of the space. The size and form of your photographs, as well as the length of the text blocks, will determine the balancing style you choose.

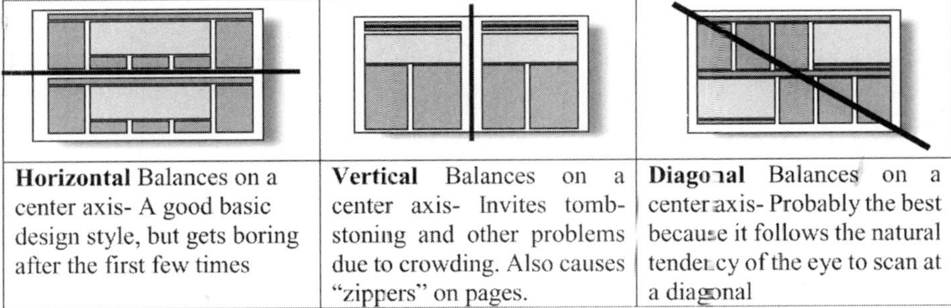

Horizontal Balances on a center axis- A good basic design style, but gets boring after the first few times	**Vertical** Balances on a center axis- Invites tomb-stoning and other problems due to crowding. Also causes "zippers" on pages.	**Diagonal** Balances on a center axis- Probably the best because it follows the natural tendency of the eye to scan at a diagonal

3. Emphasis

It gives the components and the whole the necessary weight and entails separating out what is more significant from what is less important.

4. Contrast

- It is the combining of components into one.
- Every head and cut on a page should contrast with the materials next to it.
- Adjacent headlines that are in contrast with one another will highlight the significance of the other.
- Boxes and images between the skulls are occasionally useful makeup tools.

Don'ts for layouting

1. Tomb stoning- It is the practise of aligning two or more headlines in adjacent columns such that they are about at the same level, especially if the headlines are of the same kind and point.
2. Bad breaks - tales that suddenly appear at the top of columns. Every column should have a cut or a headline at the top.
3. Separating similar images and stories.
4. Gray areas (sea of gray)- Use fillers in its place.
5. A headline that shouts at the reader is one that is too big for a brief or inconsequential story.
6. Thick tops. Avoid having a top-heavy page.
7. Arrange them all. A page shouldn't have a lot of identically sized headers.

Question Bank

1. Journalism has its birth in India in the year ________

   Ans: 1780

2. All activities concerned with the communication of mass media is not journalism.

   Ans: True

3. A ban on publication before a specific date is called as ________.

   Ans: Embargo

4. In India Journalism was started _______ state.

   Ans: West Bengal

5. The first Agricultural publication was____________ .

   Ans: Kheti

6. Newspaper editorial has a purpose of ________________

   Ans: Providing a newspaper with the chance to voice it's opinions

7. Articles are written by____________

   Ans: Newspaper and magazine reporters

8. Mass media support to Agricultural Extension scheme was launched in _______

   Ans: April 2005

9. The latest edition of the magazine is called as ___________

   Ans: Current Issue

10. The word "Cover" with reference to newspaper, means______

    Ans: Research and write the story

11. The first Agricultural journal "Transactions of Agricultural and Horticultural society of India" was published in ________.

    Ans: 1837

12. The ICAR publication- Indian Farming is ____ Publication.

    Ans: Monthly

13. Meaning of balance in a news story is _________ .

    Ans: Covering all sides of an issue as fairly as possible

14. Lithography is ________

    Ans: A method of printing

15. Spam is found in ___________

    And: Emails

16. The online places where users may participate in debates are referred to as ___________

    Ans: Forum

17. Updating the information means

    Ans: Replacing old information with the new information

18. The tool used to search the internet for information is known as the __________

    Ans: Search Function

19. The first newspaper published in India is____________

    Ans: Bengal Gazette

20. A "newsworthy" story means __________

    Ans: The story has to be about a topic that appeals to public interest

21. Personality Journalism is the other name for _________.

    Ans: Celebrity journalism

22. An Agricultural Journalist covers all the events, articles of interest and stories which are relevant to Agriculture only not allied sectors.

    Ans: False

23. Agriculture journalists report and write features that are relevant to those involved in agriculture, but stories may also be seen by non-agriculture readers.

    Ans: True

24. Newspaper is less durable than magazines.

    Ans: True

25. Crime journalism comes under the type _________

    Ans: Beat

26. Audience is the important element and the main source of news in ______ type of journalism.

    Ans: Civic Journalim

27. Precision journalism comes under ________ type of journalism.

    Ans: Information collection method

28. __________ is more advertiser driven.

    Ans: Magazine

29. _________ is a written defamation; damaging false statements against another person or institution that are in writing or are spoken from a written script

    Ans: Libel

30. _____ is a statement made by another person included in a published story.

    Ans: Quotation

31. ___________ is a form of editorial written to comment on a play, movie, piece of music or some other creative work.

    Ans: Review

32. ______ is spoken defamation; damaging false statements against another person or institution

    Ans: Slander

33. ______ is a type of story which serves to express an opinion and encourage the reader to take some action

    Ans: Editorial

34. ____________ is a standard of conduct based on moral beliefs

    Ans: Ethics

35. _________ is a statement that can be proven.

    Ans: Fact

36. ___________ is a story written with some interpretation that goes beyond just reporting the facts.

    Ans: Feature

37. Type of journalism based on writing styles are ____________

    Ans: Tabloid, Database, Graphic, Advocacy, Photo Journalism, Features

38. The kind of journalism where participants serve both the source of information and the forum for discussions and arguments is called as _____________

    Ans: Participatory

39. When many news outlets and independent reporters coordinate to produce large-scale news story, it's referred to as ______________

    Ans: Collaborative

40. Travel Journalism explains _______________

    Ans: Different parts of the world to its audience and people benefit from it in the form of getting information about various important practical details about these places, like: attractions, estimated expenditure, living facilities, food, etc.

41. _____________ played the important role in excise of freedom of expression.

    Ans: Newspapers and magazines

42. Newspapers and magazines companies are _______________

    Ans: Self-regulated

43. A news article is considered timely if it

    Ans: focuses on events that occurred today or yesterday

44. Prominence in news values refers to ____________

    Ans: how well know the people involved in the story are

45. Singularity of news story means ___________

    Ans: the reports or unusual events that diverge from the common place.

46. Hard news is __________

    Ans: about serious topics and recent events

47. Soft news is___________

    Ans: refers to human interest stories

48. Civil or public journalism is a momentum that explains ___________

    Ans: The best they can to encourage widespread participation in public affairs is what journalists should do

49. In a news story, bias is most likely to appear when

    Ans: One source is used exclusively by the reporter, or one side of the debate is given undue attention

50. Proximity of news is __________

    Ans: It happened locally

51. The name of the reporter is generally written in ______

    Ans: Byline

52. 5H & 1H is the explanation written in ___________

    Ans: Lead

53. The editor's or publisher's thoughts and opinions on specific topics or events are expressed in the section ____________

    Ans: Editorial section

54. The purpose of political cartoon is __________

    Ans: Used to provoke new perspectives on political issues and ideas

55. In a news piece, all information must be cited to the original source from which the reporter obtained it.

    Ans: True

56. Important details such as arguments, supporting data, logics, quotations, and so forth should be written in ___________

    Ans: Body

57. The least important information in the inverted pyramid structure of a news article is written in _____________

    Ans: At the end of the article

58. Magazine is derived from __________

    Ans: Arabic word

59. The world's first magazine is ___________

    Ans: Gentlemen's magazine

60. The first successful attempt for quality, up-market serious journalism in India was __________

    Ans: India today

61. Online magazines are having _______

    Ans: Linear navigation

62. Which kind of writing style spills the plot in the opening paragraph?

    Ans: Multiple inverted

63. The figurative language is used in ____________

    Ans: Imaginative writing

64. Writing persuasively demands a high level of expertise and work to persuade readers to support your position or perspective.

    Ans: True

65. The kind of writing that involves describing a character, event or a place in great details ________

    Ans: Descriptive

66. The type which includes mostly literary techniques is __________

    Ans: Narrative

67. Writing style is ________

    Ans: it is personal

68. The remaining material that was not included in the main article is referred to as ______

    Ans: Extra credit

69. Magazines are written on daily basis.

    Ans: False

70. Reduction of word count is the part of ___________

    Ans: Editing

71. The process that is performed just before the publishing is __________

    Ans: Proofreading

72. Strengthening the grammatical core of the sentence is the part of ______

    Ans: Editing

73. Readability is mainly calculated by___________

    Ans: Length of words

74. The readability of the text rely on _____

    Ans: Spacing and Punctuation

75. The make-up or window dressing of a page is called as ___________

    Ans: Layout

76. Old method of layouting is called as __________

    Ans: Conventional

77. In conventional layouting, Boxes, lines and arrows are used for ________

    Ans: Pictures/ Graphics, Headlines, Texts/ Articles respectively

78. CMYK stands for _________

    Ans: Cyan, Mangenta, Yellow and Black

79. A dummy is required for _____________

    Ans: Modern layouting

80. Placing two or more headlines on the same levelling adjacent column is called as _______

    Ans: Tomb stoning

Index